EASTER JOKES

Q: What type of eggs are easiest to stand on?

A: Eggshells!

Q: What do you call a bunny that's a king?

A: Hare to the throne!

Q: What type of egg never turns rotten?

A: Plastic ones!

Q: What do you say to a bunny looking at you funny?

A: Don't hare at me!

03

Q: What type of egg would be a convertibles?

A: A hatch back!

Q: How do bunnies celebrate New Years?

A: Happy New Ears!

04

Q: What do you call it when a kid finds an Easter egg?

A: Eggciting!

Q: What did the boy say to the chocolate Easter bunny?

A: Nice to eat you!

05

Q: Why are rabbits good at basketball?

A: They are good at making baskets.

Q: What do scary Easter eggs do?

A: Run!

Q: What do kids do with jelly beans?

A: Spill the beans!

Q: How do you tell someone how you feel about Easter?

A: Eggspress yourself!

Q: What type of basket would an Easter bunny want?

A: A 24 carrot one!

Q: What does an Easter basket without peeps say?

A: Not a peep!

Q: How would an Easter egg respond to a joke?

A: They crack up!

Q: What would peeps call their friends?

A: My peeps!

09

Q: Why does Easter scare eggs?

A: They don't wanna dye!

Q: What do you cause a plastic egg with no treat inside?

A: Bad egg!

Q: What happens when no one laughs at your easter jokes?

A: The yolks on you!

Q: How would a bunny listen to music?

A: Harepods!

Q: What do you say to a slow bunny?

A: Harry up!

Q: What are the only type of beans kids like?

A: Jelly beans!

Q: Why did the bunny not like Easter?

A: He was really a chicken!

Q: Why are bunnies good at adding?

A: Every bunny is good at simple math!

Q: What do you call rabbits that steal from other bunnies?

A: A jackrabbit!

Q: What type of filling do Easter bunnies get?

A: Caramel!

Q: What do ducks do with Easter eggs?

A: Quack them up!

Q: What happens when a bunny gets old?

A: They lose their hair!

15

Q: What would a bunny call his grandfather?

A: Hops!

Q: How would a bunny fix her hair?

A: Hare spray!

Q: Who doesn't like Easter?

A: No bunny!

Q: What time do Chickens start celebrating Easter?

A: Around the cluck!

Q: What would you eat for Easter dinner in China?

A: Egg rolls!

Q: What do you call a person begging for your easter eggs?

A: Beggar!

Q: How do you describe teaching a bunny?

A: Hare raising!

Q: How do you make Easter last forever?

A: Infinite "R"!

If you want kids to eat veggies serve them peep stew.

For Easter tell yolk yolk jokes instead.

If you have a hard time sleeping on Easter count peeps.

20

Peeps would never be allowed to hunt for eggs because of their peeping.

Bunnies are very high class they only wear 24 carrot jewelery

A week after Easter the eggs are eggstinct

If you crack an egg on your head the yolks on you.

Rabbits don't really carrot bout Easter

Knock knock
Who's there?
Bunny
Bunny who?
No bunny just me tricked you.

Knock knock
Who's there?
Heidi
Heidi who?
Heidi the eggs already let's
get the party started!

Knock knock
Who's there?
Police
Police who?
Police would you help me find
the hidden eggs.

Knock knock
Who's there?
Easter
Easter who?
Easter is a day not
a person silly!

Knock knock
Who's there?
Police
Police who?
Police would you help me find
the hidden eggs.

Knock knock
Who's there?
Bunny
Bunny who?
Very bunny aren't I

Knock knock
Who's there?
Irish
Irish who?
Irish Easter was every day.

Knock knock
Who's there?
June
June who?
June know where I can get
some glitter.

Knock knock

Who's there?

Snow

Snow who?

Snow time to play we got decorating to do.

Knock knock

Who's there?

Claus

Claus who?

Claus I can't wait til Easter

Knock knock
Who's there?
Peas
Peas who?
Peas give me more Easter Cake.

Knock knock
Who's there?
Soda
Soda who?
Soda you wanna come to my
Easter party?

Knock knock
Who's there?
Yellow
Yellow who?
Yellow are you gonna celebrate Easter?

Knock knock
Who's there?
Merry
Merry who?
Merry Easter!

Knock knock
Who's there?
Cash
Cash who?
Cash who the bunny sneezed.

Knock knock
Who's there?
Jewel
Jewel who?
Jewel be happy to know I'm inviting you this Easter.

30

Knock knock

Who's there?

Fur

Fur who?

Fur you a golden egg.

Knock knock

Who's there?

Wooden

Wooden who?

Wooden it be nice to have golden eggs.

Knock knock

Who's there?

Honey dew

Honey dew who?

Honey dew you wanna dye eggs with me.

Knock knock

Who's there?

Amish

Amish who?

Amish Easter when it's gone.

Knock knock
Who's there?
Butter
Butter who?
Butter be careful the egg will fall off the spoon.

Knock knock
Who's there?
Ketchup
Ketchup who?
Ketchup this is a sack race.

Knock knock
Who's there?
Alaska
Alaska who
Alaska again when's the Easter Party again?

Knock knock
Who's there?
Yukon
Yukon who?
Yukon start hunting now!

Knock knock
Who's there?
Olive
Olive who?
Olive Easter candy!

Knock knock
Who's there?
Weirdo
Weirdo who?
Weirdo you think the Easter
eggs are?

Knock knock
Who's there?
Dishes
Dishes who?
Dishes the Easter Bunny
speaking

Knock knock
Who's there?
Dozen
Dozen who?
Dozen anyone want to hunt
for Easter eggs

Knock knock

Who's there?

Kenya

Kenya who?

Kenya help me decorate for Easter

Knock knock

Who's there?

Tank

Tank who?

Tank you for all the Easter candy

Knock knock
Who's there?
Handsome
Handsome who?
Handsome egg dye we got
eggs to paint

Knock knock
Who's there?
Woo
Woo who?
Yeah I get pretty excited but
Easter egg hunts too

Knock knock
Who's there?
Orange
Orange who?
Orange you glad it's Easter

Knock knock
Who's there?
Needle
Needle who?
Needle little help
decorating?

Knock knock
Who's there?
Justin
Justin who?
Justin time for Easter games.

Q: What did little bear called goldilocks?

A: He said some bunny is sleeping in my bed.

Knock knock
Who's there?
Sarah
Sarah who
Sarah Easter party today?

Canoe play an Easter game
with me.

Q: What do you get when you cross an Easter egg with a snowman?

A: A Frosty the Egg-man!

Q: Why did the Easter Bunny go to the doctor?

A: He had a bad case of the hops!

Q: What did the Easter Bunny say when he met the other holiday characters?

A: "Hoppy holidays!"

Q: Why did the Easter Bunny take a nap?

A: He was egg-hausted!

43

Q: What do you call an Easter Bunny with a fever?

A: A hot cross bunny!

Q: How does the Easter Bunny get around so fast?

A: By using his hare-raising speed!

Q: How does the Easter Bunny keep his fur looking so nice?

A: He uses hare spray!

Q: What's the best way to make Easter easier?

A: Put an "i" where the "t" is.

Knock, knock!
Who's there?
Butcher.
Butcher who?
Butcher eggs in the basket!

Q: Where does Christmas come before Easter?

A: The dictionary!

Q: What do you get when you pour boiling water into a rabbit hole?

A: Hot cross bunnies!

Knock. knock!
Who's there?
Heidi.
Heidi who?
Heidi the eggs all around the backyard!

47

Q: Why is the Easter Bunny so lucky?

A: Because he has four rabbits feet!

Q: How does every Easter end?

A: With an "r!"

48

Q: What kind of stories do Easter eggs like to tell their children?

A: Yolk tales.

Knock. knock!
Who's there?
Wendy.
Wendy who?
Wendy Easter egg hunt gonna start?

Q: What do you get when you cross a rabbit with shellfish?

A: An oyster bunny!

Q: How do you send a letter to the Easter Bunny?

A: By hare mail.

50

Q: What's invisible and smells like carrots?

A: A bunny fart!

Q: What do you call the Easter Bunny the Monday after Easter?

A: Eggs-hausted.

Knock, knock!
Who's there?
Some bunny.
Some bunny who?
Some bunny's been hiding
my Easter eggs!

Q: What did one Easter egg say
to the other?

A: "Heard any good yolks today?"

Q: What is the Easter Bunny's favorite kind of music?

A: Hip-hop!

Q: Why shouldn't you tell an Easter egg a joke?

A: It might crack up!

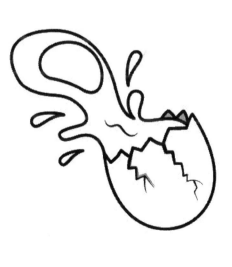

Q: What happened when the Easter Bunny met the rabbit of his dreams?

A: They lived hoppily ever after.

Q: What kind of jewelry do rabbits wear?

A: 14 carrot gold.

Q: How does the Easter Bunny stay fit?

A: Eggs-ercise!

Q: What do you call a mischievous egg?

A: A practical yolker.

Q: Why was the Easter Bunny upset?

A: He was having a bad hare day.

Q: What did the Easter Bunny say to the carrot?

A: It's been nice gnawing you.

Q: What do you call a line of rabbits jumping backwards?

A: A receding hare-line.

Q: Where does the Easter Bunny go when he needs a new tail?

A: To a re-tail store!

Q: What happened to the Easter Bunny when he misbehaved at school?

A: He was eggspelled!

Q: How does the Easter Bunny keep his fur looking good?

A: With a hare brush!

Q: What do you call a rabbit with fleas?

A: Bugs Bunny!

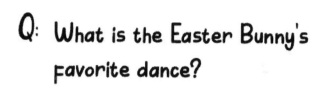

Q: What is the Easter Bunny's favorite dance?

A: The bunny hop!

59

Q: It's true that bunnies have have good eyesight?

A: You never see a bunny wearing glasses, after all!

Knock, knock!

Who's there?

Alma.

Alma who?

Alma Easter candy is gone. Can I have some more?

60

Q: What did the Easter Bunny say about the Easter parade?

A: It was eggs-cellent!

Q: What is the Easter Bunny's favorite sport?

A: Basket-ball of course!

61

Q: Did you hear the one about the Easter Bunny who sat on a bee?

A: It's a tender tail!

Q: Where does the Easter Bunny get his eggs?

A: From an eggplant!

62

Q: What do you call a rabbit who makes good jokes?

A: A funny bunny!

Q: What kind of stories do Easter bunnies like best?

A: Ones with hoppy endings!

Q: Why did the new egg feel so good?

A: Because he just got laid!

Q: What did the doctor tell the chicken with high cholesterol?

A: "Try to lay off eggs for a while!"

64

Q: What do you call a
smart omelet?

A: An egg head!

Q: How did the omelet find
out she was ill?

A: She had a medical eggs-am!

Q: Where can you go to learn more about eggs?

A: The hen-cyclopedia!

Q: How do you make an egg roll?

A: Just give it a little push!

Q: What did the egg do when it saw the frying pan?

A: It scrambled!

Q: Why don't rabbits get hot in the summer?

A: They have hare conditioning.

Q: Why did the Easter Bunny hide his eggs?

A: He was egg-secuting his duties!

Q: Why did the Easter egg hide in the refrigerator?

A: It wanted to chill out!

Q: What did the Easter egg say to its girlfriend?

A: "You're the yolk of my life!"

Q: Why was the Easter Bunny so bad at painting eggs?

A: Because he only had one brush-tail!

Made in the USA
Columbia, SC
04 April 2023

14747840R00039